LIFE

in black & white

Dear Phil,
    Very best wishes,
        Love, Kathlea

Hope you enjoy this
book of short stories &
poetry written by Kathleen
        Anne Marie
    (Christmas 2014)

Catherine Thorne

KEEPER BOOKS

1

Published 2014 by KEEPER BOOKS
through FeedARead.com
with funding from
the English Arts Council

First Edition

A CIP catalogue record for this title is available from the British Library

Paperbacks and eBooks are available from –

FeedAread.com
Amazon.co.uk
Amazon.com

Booksellers can order from –

Ingrams; Barnes & Noble; Easons;
Gardners; Nielsen; Bertrams, Argosy

Contents

In memory
of
my brother

John J Madden

Preface

LET me warn anyone who picks up this little book that it has no pretensions whatever to literary merit. It is merely a collection of personal musings and stories. The stories are fictional but some are based on happenings in an Ireland that bears little resemblance to this 21st-century Ireland of ours.

I was cajoled, pushed and bullied into putting it together, primarily by my partner and mentor, David Rice. Without David's support I would never have touched a computer much less have written anything.

Now that it's done I am grateful - not because it will ever appear in a bookshop or market stall, but because somewhere down the line it will provide a small indication of the fact that I once existed.

Thank you, David.

~ Catherine Thorne
Ballina
Killaloe
September 2014

A red-leather purse

When she died,
Her red-leather purse
 cowered,
Dull and lifeless
 on the mantelpiece,
Brass catch stiff, unyielding.
Inside, the shabby pennies
 and the shillings
Gathered grit.

Grief ached then
For a loss –

Forever buried

In memories

That whisper

To console,

But lack the life

Of living fingers

To polish,

To count the pennies,

To restore to living

A red leather purse

A Hare

Fifty years ago

A hare in madness raced

Thumping and thudding

Down the middle

Of a tarmac road.

Shocked or stunned

I gaped and marvelled

At the power of its hind legs.

I see it still,

Like the wild rush

Of a notion,

Taking hold

In a moment

Of mad abandon

Abundance

I'm really not that good at all.
I do not climb Croagh Patrick
Barefoot at the crack of dawn.
I do not fast and beat my breast
Or shake my beads and mumble prayers
Before the bleeding heart of Jesus.

I sit and stare at sweeping
        flocks of starlings.
I listen to the swish of winds

in winter trees.
I cuddle my hairy dog and
scratch her belly.
I drink red wine and eat
good cheese.
In truth, I love to wallow
in life's abundance

Fresh bread*

'THAT'S the smell of bread in the oven, Mammy.'

'Yes, love.'

'But you never bake, Mammy.'

'I used to, lovey, when your Dad and I first got married.'

'Why did you stop? I love Granny's bread.'

This stung Maud. 'Stop asking so many questions. I just felt like it. Go out and play and leave me alone.'

---

* Shortlisted for the Hennessy Award in 2001

The small girl climbed off the stool under the window. Unperturbed. 'Can we have some at teatime? And jam, Granny's strawberry jam?'

'That's what we bake bread for, isn't it, to eat it?'

The child scampered out to the yard.

The splutter of a tractor sounded in the distance, getting louder. She looked at the clock. The men would soon be in for tea. She gasped for breath as she felt the pleasure in her belly and felt her nipples tighten.

I never thought to feel like this again, she thought.

And then she thought of her husband; her suitable, well-off farmer husband - in Brussels now to talk about subsidies, quotas and set-asides. He worked hard and sometimes she exasperated him, she knew.

'Christ, woman, have you no interest at all in this farm. You haven't listened to a word I've said. It's your bread and butter, you know.'

Bread and butter.

'Why can't you bake decent bread? Can't you do anything right! Go over to my mother and she'll show you.'

'Granny bakes lovely bread. I wanted to bring you some but she said you wouldn't like it.'

Granny was so perfect!

The oven alarm sounded, snapping Maud out of her reverie. The bread looked good. She tapped the bottom of the cake for the hollow sound that said it was baked. It would be cooler but still warm enough to melt butter when the men came in.

'We must feed the men when they come to work. It's the tradition here,' her husband had told her years ago. And she *had* fed them. At ploughing, shearing or harvest, they came in droves. She was a dutiful wife. She was bound to this place, to the mud, the smells of animals, the isolation.

'It's not an easy life,' her mother-in-law had said. 'And the hardest bit will be finding your own life here.'

Her own life: friends, books, clothes, job; all gone. She had loved Richard from the comfort of her own life. A handsome farmer, mover and shaker in the IFA, full of concern for his mother when his father had died. She would follow him anywhere and did, to this midland place of flat boredom.

The splutter of the tractor again, closer now. They're working their way towards their tea. He would be driving. He was blond and tanned with the tiniest scar on his left cheek.

'Mammy, when is Daddy coming home?' The child was back in the kitchen again.

'Tomorrow night. I've told you that before. Why do you keep asking?'

The child sat on the ground in front of a bookcase.

'Will he bring us presents, Mammy? You never wore the earrings he brought you the last time. I hope he brings me books.'

Those earrings, lovely, expensive and chosen with love. But what good were they in this god-forsaken place of mud and misery?

Except maybe today.

A dog came to the kitchen door, head down, body waggling, tail wagging. The child saw the dog and raised her arms to hug him. The dog crept to her, to a moment's pleasure in the child's arms.

'Get that filthy animal out of here,' Maud screamed.

Dog and child ran from the kitchen.

The tractor was in the yard. She ran to the sideboard; must set the table. The kettle was boiling. He would be in the kitchen in a matter of minutes. He would look at her with intense blue eyes. She would look away, heart racing, unable to think.

Did he feel something for her? Big age gap. But still she was attractive, had kept her figure. She looked young in her jeans and tee shirt. Her nipples were tingling, standing out like little bullets under the soft cotton of the tee shirt. Her husband liked that. He used to tease her and pinch them in the early days.

The clock in the hall chimed four. This young farm manager was a strict time-keeper. His references had all said that. Keen, efficient, polite, punctual. Couldn't have been better.

'You needn't worry about anything, love,' her husband had said a week ago.' I think we've got a good one this time.'

She hadn't expected him to be quite so good, so beautiful to look at. She longed for her own youth, some fun.

She saw him through the kitchen window. Taller than the other men. Red sweater and blue jeans. He had taken off the overalls. The others had done the same. He was a leader: they respected him. They stood together, five of them, a multicoloured bunch, some smoking cigarettes, some drinking cola.

He did neither. His blond hair stood out above the others. When he laughed, his teeth shone brilliant white in the sunlight. A song came to her from her youth. *The Bee Gees*. She saw the TV advertisement that went with it, young people singing and waving:

> I'd like to teach the world to sing
> In perfect harmony
> Grow apple trees and honey bees
> And snow white turtle doves.

She turned to the aga to make the tea. Her back would be to the door when they came in. One of the Aga lids was sticking a little. Maybe she would call him at the end to unstick it for her- a thought.

She finished pouring the water into the teapot. They were a little slower than usual coming in. Something was amusing them, delaying them. She fiddled with her earrings. One of them was loose; fasten it - an excuse to look in the mirror! Fix her hair, adjust her bra. Her colour was higher than she liked. A little dab of moisturiser on each cheek to cool her down.

'What are you doing, Mammy, is your face sore?'

Maud jumped. She had forgotten the child.

'No, lovey, just a little hot from the cooker.'

'You look funny.'

The kitchen door opened. He came first as usual; exuberant, smiling. They were all smiling, vibrant, physical.

'Mrs Ryan, gorgeous as always. Fresh bread, great.'

They took their places at the table. Some confidently grabbed chairs, unaware of social niceties; others hung back, polite. He sat at the top where her husband sat. She poured the tea. The child sidled up to one of the older men. She was showing him some pictures in a book. The dog slunk in between window and table.

She saw him looking at her breasts. Her nipples were stiff, almost sore with stiffness. He had guessed. She would keep her dignity but she knew he had guessed. She would ask him about the aga lid. Then, maybe he would touch her.

She put the tea pot back on the Aga. The men's conversation began to take off in thick, ugly sounds, between mouthfuls of her fresh bread. They were ignoring her.

'Have you finished the bottom field?' she asked. Silence. The question had shocked herself into silence.

'But they were doing the middle field, Mammy. That's what Daddy said they were to do today,' the child said.

Maud curbed the urge to send the child out of the room.

'Of course, how stupid of me.'

'We start the bottom field tomorrow, Mrs Ryan. That will be it then. Job done. Mr Ryan will be back tomorrow, I believe.'

'Yes,' the child piped up, 'and he'll bring us presents. I know what he's going to bring Mammy.'

They all guffawed. Including him. The child looked stunned. Maud felt sorry for her and went to hold her. She squirmed out of her grasp and ran from the room. Maud followed her but only went as far as the sitting room. She would recover her composure. She was angry. How dare they laugh at a child's innocence! Crude insolence!

Her sitting room was elegant, calm. The sun shone through the french window. Outside the roses were a riot of vivid colours. She opened the french window to let in some air. The tall beech trees stood strong and majestic around the lawn. How dare they make her feel cheap! They sat in there eating her fresh bread, laughing at her. She would not face them again.

Then he called from the kitchen door, 'We're off now, Mrs Ryan. Lovely bread. Thank you very much.'

She remained silent. He was gone. Just the roses, sunshine and trees. Then the child and dog crossed the lawn on their way to the orchard. There would be apples there now for her to eat and the dog to play with. Maybe I'll make an apple tart for Richard tomorrow, she thought.

A man is shot

A man is shot in Moyross.

A child is abducted in Dublin.

A suicide bomber in Baghdad

Straps his deadly cargo to himself.

Histories of miseries convulse

In each act of desperation

In each moment of vindication

Of aspiration

Of exasperation.

Powerless I watch.

I search for meaning

In the depths of memory,

In the convoluted rationalities

Of histories repeated,

Of stories told,

'Till fogs yellow as bile

Confuse,

And fracture the thin film

Of life's daily dalliance

With meanings

In the meaningless confusions

Of lives lived and loved

In the quagmires of fear and despair.

And yet,

Despite it all

We feather our nests

We breed and gather our brood

And tell them stories and histories

In the hope that,

In the end,

It will all come right

A night in summer

In a night of glistening lights and sparkling
river
Noise rises from the town below –
Now a shriek, then a roar.
A car rips a track through Quarry Lane,
A song bursts free on a gust
Of night-time exuberance
By a river's edge.

History lurks in Boru's hill
In the stones of a bridge arched and
crumbling,
In a tower, erect and proud
From long dominion over right and wrong,
In cemeteries heaped with the detritus of
dead dreams.

A sharp sliver of a new moon
Eyes the night and blinks,
As clouds dim its silver sheen.

A bat flits, splitting a second.
A dog barks at her own echo.
A suicidal moth whacks the light bulb,
As late-night songs roll on the wind.

A woman sits and sips her wine -
Detached in a moment,
Of history's continuum,
        As a night rings with Summer living

A red knitted sock

I KNOW your story well now, Mary Convey. But for years I only knew your red knitted sock in a drawer in my grandmother's dressing table. It hung on rusted needles and I marvelled at its even stitching, its bright-red colour and the warmth of its wool in my child hands.

'Who owns this, Gran?'

'Who made this, Mammy?'

'Daddy, can I play with the needles and red sock?'

The answer was always the same:

'Put that away and mind your own business.'

But how could I put it away – something so beautiful! Someone had achieved what the teacher had failed to teach me – even stitching, a perfectly turned heel and it was red. I loved red, but Mammy would never let me wear red. More than anything I had wanted a red jumper or a red dress but no, it clashed with my red hair she said.

That sock drew me to it like a butterfly to a nettle until one day my mother snapped in anger and said, 'Mary Convey made it.'

And who was Mary Convey, I wondered. Soon, answers came more easily. You were my granny's cousin and you had lived your whole life in the village of Ballina. My dad told me that you had never been to Limerick, much less Dublin. But why did nobody want to talk about you and show your beautiful knitting to the whole world?

One day my mother let it slip, 'Do you know what your father did the minute he came into the nursing home when you were born? He stripped back the clothes and examined your feet.'

He examined my baby feet, Mary, because you were pigeon toed. You were a flawed creature. You pigeon toes were a blight on the image of a strong family. You were their shame. That shame sat on your shoulders and bent you like a hawthorn bush in the path of the north wind.

You shuffled your way up and down the village. You turned to look at a shop window when you saw someone coming. At the draper's, Pakie Mack looked out over an expensive dress and scoffed. He hated the Conveys and was glad to see their bad luck made flesh in your pigeon toes. Some people were used to you and spoke of the weather and the price of bread and whether someone was ill or dying or maybe a baby was due in some family.

You visited my grandmother. She was kind to you. She loved you. You knitted suits, gloves, hats and scarves for my father when he was born. Did you think then of the baby that might have been yours? But no man looked at your tiny figure hunched over a walking stick as you shuffled to Mass or the shops or over the bridge to Killaloe to visit your cousins.

You wore long skirts and a black cloak. You hid your beautiful hair under a hood of heavy tweed. Young boys were cruel. 'Did you ever see a crab, Mary? Pluck off their claws and they grow again.'

You bowed your head and shuffled on. Did you curse your father for the strange fish he caught and brought home before you were born? Your mother screamed, 'Take it out. It'll harm the baby.'

You were born with your toes turned in and your mother blamed the fish. But your father was a fisherman and fish meant food and life. 'God bless us, woman, how could you say such a thing?'

They said little to each other after that. A silence entered your house then – the silence of resentment. You were a punishment from God. You stayed at home - you were kept at home. No school, no friends. But your aunt took pity on you and taught you how to knit. You learned well.

They came from miles around for winter socks and long-johns. Your fingers worked magic on the best yarns from Limerick, and bainin from Ennis.

'The cripple will knit me a scarf. The cripple can use her hands.'

God had stolen from you but he had also given. You would survive and live in your father's house long after his death and your mother's.

The smells from Ryan's bakery next door woke you in the mornings. Kelly's cows passed through the bow-way to the farmyard behind the house. You were up then, busy with your needles and counting the stitches.

Women came for their socks and mittens. 'I'll bring the money on Friday, Mary,' some would say. But you had learnt and knew to reply, 'No money, no socks. I have to buy my needles and thread.'

You earned well and ate well. You wore good tweed skirts and blouses of the best lawn. You heard the whispers: 'look at the cripple in her fancy skirts. What gives her such notions?'

Shoes were your problem. James Lafferty was the only shoemaker for miles round who could measure and shape the leather of the soft boots that would carry your shuffling in comfort.

It was Mrs Ryan who liked red. Her daughters wore red skirts, red jumpers, red gloves, red socks. She couldn't get enough red. You counted the stitches of her reds garments and measured her shillings into pots for new winter boots and warm flannel for a petticoat. You were sure of Mrs Ryan. Her husband owned the bakery and the bakery made money in a parish of sodden bogs and black peat.

They eyed you and hated your comfort. They squinted and told stories of a fish with the head of a woman. They opened the cupboard of the sins of your father and his father. They cut them, dissected them, tasted them and spat them from mouth to ear across bog and stone and felt good in their sure-footed hunger.

Black peat fired the ovens that baked the bread in Ryan's bakery. It dried your house and warmed your bones.

You heard Tom Ryan whistling that morning. He's drinking whiskey again you knew. And that was your last thought before heaven opened and gathered its wounded fish from a sea of smoke in a drunken fire of dried out peat and wood.

They found your suffocated body curled in a warm heap of red wool and steel needles.

My father uncurled your bones and laid you out in your smoke stained house beside the burnt out shell of Ryan's bakery. He took your last, unfinished sock and put it in his mother's drawer.

It lay there for me to play with, wonder about and know your life of shuffling misery in a world that threw you out and measured your worth in knitted socks and turned-in toes.

A tangled web

A tangled web of origins, destinations

Requirements or sufficiencies

Binds me to living,

In thrall to beauty,

To love of life,

Toward a destiny

Where I repay

Earth's bounty

In the cycle of another's life

Through death

Or resurrection

To renewed living

In endless rebirth

Absence

The phone rings.

I think

It could be you.

But then I know

Your silence.

Deeper now

Than life's reluctant speech.

More eloquent now

Than failures to explain.

In the silence

I hear your joy

Like a great burst of birds

In the wheeling frenzy

Of an evening sky.

I hear your pain

In the anvil bell

Of the blacksmith's fiery blow.

A robin teck-tecks

A note so old

It needs no clear defining.

An old church bell

Tells tales

Of shuffling shoes

And mumbling prayers

As life settles

To your hollow absence

An oar

An oar stands upright
In our backyard.
Smooth, blue and cut with the grain
Of timber worthy
Of life on the river.

Good fishing today,
An hour on the river, it says.
Waters smooth or rough
Yielded to its plunge
At the power of my father's behest.

Dapping or angling,
It cut the flood
To the seasonal rhythms
Of mayfly or worm.

It promised
An eel for the dinner,
A trout for the supper,
Or only a perch today.

A picnic on Holy Island
Where ancient monks sang Vespers
Through the gold
Of a setting sun.

Against a sudden gust at Parker's Point,
Before mighty winds
Or savage current
It stoutly held its own.

It stands erect now,
Smooth and blue,

With a notch at its tip

To prop up the clothesline

And stage the squawking

Of hungry crows

An old ship

An old ship lists

Offering a rusty hulk

To a hungry sea.

Not enough water to float her,

To rescue her

From abandonment.

A curlew flies above her.

It banks and dares a bitter wind.

It glides towards the blue Atlantic,

To skies where vapour-trails

Penetrate a golden dawn.

Eternity glistens above me.

Death rusts below me

The bat

THE young nun was tired. God, a break, please. A hot gruelling day it had been. Teaching, lunch supervision, scarcely time to eat her own lunch, teaching and the never-ending demands of young girls and their parents.

Prayers over, she left the chapel. Dear God, no chatting this evening, no company, just peace and quiet, please. The chapel door clicked shut behind her. A quick glance: no one around!

A soft breeze blew up from the river. Clouds of pollen drifted across the meadow. She headed straight for the gravel path to the little bridge.

She would stand there and bathe in the sound of the gushing rapids.

The convent dog, almost blind, sensed her presence. One comfort at least. Fat and soft, he snuggled up to her thigh and licked her hand. A little comfort for him, too.

Several turnstiles blocked the path. 'They control movement,' the old nun had told her. What movement? She didn't know. She never asked.

I'd love to run down that hill, she thought, looking at the sharp descent to the river.

An image struck her -- the image of a young, free girl in tee-shirt and shorts, hair flowing loose and the joy of the warm sun on bare arms and legs, and then to dive in the cool clear water of another river. A long time ago, that was.

They reached the first turnstile. Stiff and heavy, but brilliant in a coat of new white paint, the gate yielded a few inches to let her through. The dog squeezed through the bottom two wires of the fence and wobbled on in front of her. A grove of tall beech trees on their right now blocked her view of the convent. She stopped to look.

Lush rich meadow, water sparkling under a low sun. Bird song counterpoint to the rush of the river. She raised her face to the sun-- felt its soft heat and laughed at the thought of the freckles so despised by her grandmother.

The warmth had not reached far through the grove of trees. Dark and dank in there, it made her shiver. Then a quick flash of turquoise - a kingfisher.

Distracted by the lucky glimpse, she moved towards the second turnstile. The dog had already reached the fence beside it, his nose pointing towards the top strand of wire. His broad yellow back quivered, his tail wagged rapidly. H e was interested in something. She was curious.

There, hanging by its toes from the wire, was a bat. She was astonished. A bat shouldn't be here. Surely they slept in dark places during the day?

Weren't they creatures of the night? Old lore came to her. They swooped through the air - built-in radar - no colliding or crashing. So her father had told her. Her mother had told her they could get caught in her hair and if they did she'd never get them out. Rubbish, her father had said. Now she wasn't sure.

She put her hand to her head. A veil covered her hair. Protected by the veil - a veil the symbolised her breach with the world and covered her crown of red curly hair. It would now save her from the bat. Poor bat, stiff and rigid, terrified. Not a move out of it. The dog kept his distance, respectful, unsure.

She looked a long time. The dog lost interest and sat panting. She sat on the grassy slope between trees and meadow. The tiny mouse-head showed no signs of life. Filmy lids covered its eyes. Could it be dead?

Shrill screams and laughter came from the hockey field. A car drove down the avenue towards the main road - a lay teacher on her way home. Stabs of envy bit at the young nun's gut. She imagined the teacher at home, greeting her husband, hugging the children, evening meal, snug by the fire before bedtime.

The dog rolled over on his back. Scratch my belly, his kicking legs said. Shoes cast off, she rubbed her soles on the soft hair of the fat dog's belly. Warm, soft, yielding flesh, happy in a moment's pleasure. The bat hung still and rigid, a tiny life alone on a foreign fence.

'Sister, sister!' a girl's voice called.

God in heaven, will they never leave me alone?

'Sister, sister!'

God give me peace.

The bat hung upside down, immobile. At peace? Surely not, in a place so alien. It engrossed her now. Old lore and fears vanished. What should she do - prise open the little claws and let him free? The fright would kill him. She moved closer to look. Her nose almost touched the bat's claw. She gently blew the soft warmth of her breath on it. A slight movement. She blew again. a stronger movement. She started back, a little alarmed. What if it flew at her, turned on her, misjudged her motives? It hung still again.

Around her the evening air breathed freely. Warm and fragrant, with the life of grass and trees and birds; it enveloped and oppressed her.

A young girl in tee-shirt and shorts stood beside her, out of breath.

'A bad cut on Jane's knee, Sister. Come quick!'

'Isn't Sister Bride on duty?'

'But she hates blood. Please come, Sister.'

'Wrap a towel round it. I'll be there in a while.'

The dog's nose was touching the bat's head, pushing a little, very gently. She grabbed his collar and pulled him off the fence. 'Leave it alone, you bad dog. Poor little bat.'

The dog looked offended but lay down and rolled on his back.

One of the older nuns came walking towards her from the convent. 'They're all looking for you, Sister,' she said. 'Something wrong on the hockey field.'

'But I'm not on duty, Sister. Sister Bride is there.'

'On duty, off duty. What does it matter here?' said the nun, and continued stiffly towards the river.

The young nun had thought to show her the bat, but didn't. No reason. She just didn't.

She stayed sitting. The bat hung, undisturbed by light or dog or noise. Is that the way to do it? Sit it out and it will all go away. She had a sudden longing to take the veil off her head and shake her hair out in the freshness of the evening air. She looked at the bat again, and then whipped off the veil.

A solemn moment from the day of her profession came to her. One nun deftly slipping off the white veil of the novice, while another pinned on the black veil of the professed nun. She would wear it for the rest of her life as a sign of her vows.

She was defiant now. There was pleasure in the touch of the warm air on her neck and ears and through her red hair. She shook her head and rubbed her fingers through the short frizzy strands. I've broken a rule, she thought. The bat hung still.

The dog sniffed the abandoned veil. Oh God, he might run away with it. She grabbed it. She held it for another minute then shook her head again. It felt so good -- the freedom of it.

'Sister, Sister!'

She saw the round figure of Sister Bride waddling past the chapel windows and heading in her direction. A moment of hesitation. The young nun sat still, face to the sun, freckles bedamned. She laughed to herself. The dog nosed the bat. The bat swayed a little, but held on tight to the wire.

Sister Bride huffed and puffed her way through the turnstile and down the gravel path towards her. 'Sister!' she called again.

'Yes, Sister?' the young nun replied.

Then Sister Bride saw her. She stood aghast, taking in the sight of the bare head and the red hair. She covered her mouth with one hand, turned on her heel and scurried back up the path.

Auschwitz I

March 2009

I tried to enter that dark space
Through the cold of bitter memory,
Through the mounds of relics
Caged now in clean glass cases,
Through the dead beauty of
A baby's pink smocked dress,
Through a kangaroo court-room

And slaughtering yard,

Through cells of hellish hope

In the despair of just not knowing,

Through a million spectacles

Deprived of eyes in fires so fierce

They ate the soul.

And then I think of Abraham

Hand poised to kill his son

When love not law supremely superseded

Auschwitz II

Words died in me

When I found no word

To sound

The depths of evil

In a black chasm

At the heart

Of a depravation

That knows not depravation

But bursts the boundaries

Of death's last word

'Father forgive them for they know
not what they do.'

No answer came
To them forsaken
Beneath the darkest cloud
In hell's domain

Auschwitz III

Memory capers a fast track

To retributions and newish tribulations

Where love lies buried in mounds

Of justifications

In a story retold, relived

In worlds without end. Amen

Birth

A new moon shimmers in a black sky.

A new rose buds on an old stalk.

The root that birthed a thousand blooms

Defies the gnarled death of winter's depths

To loosen the juicy freshness

In a bud so small

Its blood-red petals hesitate

To grasp the warmth of spring's new sun

And join the riotous living

Of summer's symphony to life

Christmas Eve

IT'S hard to imagine the events of a few short hours on Christmas Eve could have changed the outlook of an old woman. There's no doubt about it but, at the age of sixty-nine, I had thought of myself as over the hill and on the last run to the field at the back of the church. But not now. I feel vigorous in myself again and I'm no longer the depressed old granny who set out for the train to spend Christmas with her daughter and family in Dublin.

My neighbour Jack Hehir dropped me off at the station with a comfortable ten minutes to spare before the three-o'clock train. Everything was going like clockwork. There was nobody but myself travelling and I got my ticket without the slightest trouble.

I looked at my watch and decided I'd have time enough to go to the toilet before the train pulled in. I pushed my bag in under the seat near the ticket office and set off to the small shed at the other end of the long platform

Such an uncomfortable, smelly little box of a place. But then, what would you expect from a country station with an idiot like Paddy Moran looking after it. He calls himself The Station Master, if you don't mind! While the same fellow would mind mice at the crossroads for you if there was money in it, he'd be too stupid to see the filth under his nose. Even the flush toilet didn't work properly.

I was just thinking that I'd need disinfecting after such a place, when I put my had up to open the door. It was one of those bolts on a kind of roller and the blasted thing was stuck. It wouldn't budge for me. I pulled it and shoved it. I rattled the door and kicked it. Could that bloody fool get nothing right in this god-forsaken place?

Then I began to get worried about the time. The train was due in at any minute. I shouted, 'Paddy Moran, come up here and let me out!' I might as well have been calling my own poor Paddy back out of the grave.

Then I heard the train. I could feel my heart racing in my chest. What If I collapse with an angina pain? I searched in my pocket for a tablet. Dearest God - I'd left them in my bag near the ticket window. I banged on the door as hard as I could. I screamed and shouted. I kicked the door again and again. I stood up on the toilet seat to see if I had any hope of climbing over the door. Not a chance.

By this time the train had screamed to a halt outside. That fool of a Paddy Moran would never hear me now. And this was the last train to Dublin before the Christmas. I started to cry. I heard the blast of the horn and then the train pulling out of the station. What was I going to do? That fellow would go home and leave me here for the whole Christmas. I gathered what strength I had left in me and started kicking and banging and shouting again.

Then I heard footsteps and somebody say, 'I'm sure there's someone in there. Listen again.'

I thumped and screamed. Then: 'What are you doing in there, Mrs Moody? I thought you got on the train.'

'Open the door, you bloody fool!' I shouted. That was strong language from me. I'm not a swearing woman.

I could nearly hear the cogs in his poor slow brain starting to turn. 'I'll get a screwdriver,' he finally decided.

By now it wasn't the smell and the filth of the place that were worrying me. I sat down on the toilet seat and cried my heart out. I hadn't really wanted to go to Dublin in the first place, but arrangements had been made. Now I'd have to go back home and face Christmas Day with nothing in the house for the dinner.

When Moran finally let me out I hit him a thump in the chest. Not that it made the slightest impact on his huge, padded bulk. But then a strange thing happened: his sheer stupidity had a calming effect on me. 'I'll look after you, Mam,' he said.

Then, as if to prove he was mad as well as stupid, he took off to run out of the station and up the short hill to the main road. I was left looking after him with my mouth open. Next I saw him standing nearly in the middle of the road wildly waving his arms in the direction of the oncoming traffic.

Almost immediately a huge lorry pulled in and he ran to talk to the driver. Soon he was racing back down to the station shouting, 'I've got a lift for you! I've got a lift for you!' He grabbed my bag with one hand and my arm with the other and wheeled me in the direction of the lorry. I was speechless.

I had never in my life seen the insides of a lorry, much less taken a lift in one. As I got near the monster its sheer height made me nervous. I'd never manage to get up those steps into the cab. They were nearly vertical. But before I could shout stop, my bag was airborne and had landed on the floor beside the driver. And there was I with a bearded young man pulling me by the arms and my backside being pushed by Paddy Moran. Before I could even think of indignity, I was sitting high above the road beside a total stranger, with Paddy waving goodbye and shouting, 'Happy Christmas, Mrs Moody.'

What had I got myself into? For a while I could see the driver watching me out of the corner of his eye. He said nothing for ages. Then, as if reading my thoughts and sensing my anxiety he said, 'I'll have you at Heuston before the train, you know, Ma'am.'

That at least was a relief. Then he began to be concerned for my comfort and made sure I had enough heat and air. He usually like to keep the cab a little cool for himself, he explained. It kept him more alert.

This seemed a nice young man and the view of the countryside from the unaccustomed height was proving interesting. I found myself beginning to relax and enjoy myself. He had a tape on, playing Christmas carols very softly. I was thankful it wasn't loud modern music that would blast the head off an elephant. I'd have enough of that to put up with in Dublin from the grandchildren. And besides, thank God I hadn't spent €20 of my own money to swell the coffers of Iarnrod Eireann. This was better than any free travel by train. And I wouldn't have the trouble of changing at Ballybrophy.

By the time we got to Nenagh I had become so comfortable in myself that I began to wonder about who this young man was, and why he was out on the road with such a big lorry on Christmas Eve.

'I had to make an emergency delivery of animal feed to Cork yesterday,' he told me.

This made sense. It had been an unusually hard winter so far and the grass on the land had run out sooner than the farmers had expected. We talked a bit about farming and, for a Dubliner, his knowledge of all things rural surprised me. I didn't like to ask too many personal questions, but I put two and two together when he told me he has spend the night with his aunt in Lisnagry.

'So your family comes from around here?' I asked.

'Yes. My father was born and reared on a farm just outside Newport.'

I was really interested now. It turned out that he had spent many of his childhood summers with his grandparents on the family farm and loved this part of the country.

We talked a bit about Newport and the Clare Glens. It turned out that before he picked me up he had visited both places and felt 'refreshed for the Christmas', as he put it. This was a most unusual young man indeed. Most of the young fellows I knew would think themselves consigned to some outer darkness if they found themselves anywhere other than a pub on Christmas Eve.

After a while I ventured to ask him his name. When he told me he was Michael McGrath, I was dumbfounded. 'Would your father be Michael McGrath from outside Newport?' I asked.

'Yes. Did you know him?'

Did I *what*. Great Lord above, did I ever know Michael McGrath from outside Newport? Didn't I fancy him for the best part of my young life? At least, that is, until he left home to join the Civil Service. And even then it took me years to root him out of my mind and heart. Of course I couldn't tell this to his son in one fell swoop, so my reply was a guarded, 'Yes, I knew him well when we were young.'

I suppose my voice gave me away, because I saw him again looking at me out of the corner of his eye and he was smiling. I was embarrassed but thrilled to hear about Mick after all these years. It took me a while to compose myself and work up the courage to pursue this matter a little further. 'I suppose your father has retired by now?'

'Well, yes and no,' was the reply. 'He's still the brains behind this business, but he doesn't put in as many hours as he used to.'

That made me sit up. 'When did he leave the Civil Service?' I asked.

'Oh, that was long before I was born. Somehow I could never imagine Dad in a desk job. He's still bursting with energy. Only he used some of it now on the golf course and shouting at football matches.'

The idea of golf was a little foreign to me, but many's the hurling and football match I had followed Mick to, all those years ago. It's far from matches I am nowadays, God knows, but it was great to hear that Mick was in such great form.

I had always been curious to know who Mick had married, so now was my chance. 'And what about your mother - does she go to the matches with him?

'Poor Mam, she was never much interested in Dad's sporting activities,' he said gently. 'She died, you know, three years ago.'

I was genuinely shocked to hear this. 'Was she buried in Dublin?' I asked, knowing well that if she had been brought back to Newport I'd probably have heard something about it.

'Yes. She's buried in the family plot in Glasnevin.'

Then I got courage to probe a little further. 'Did she come from around there?'

'Dublin born and bred.' He clammed up then and I knew that that was all I was going to hear about his mother, for the time being, at any rate.

When we got to Portlaoise he asked me if I'd like to stop for coffee. I baulked at the idea of descending from this vehicle unnecessarily, and then having to climb back in again.

'No problem at all,' said my companion. He pulled into the large forecourt of a pub on the Dublin side of the town and like a shot was out of the lorry and over to the door on my side. 'Turn your back to me now, and grab those handles.'

I did as he said and, for the second time on this holy day, I found my backside being grabbed by the strong hands of a young man. Just as well my poor Paddy was in his grave. He was always a bit on the jealous side.

We had a great chat about family and friends over coffee. The longer I knew him, the easier it was to talk to him. I always like to look a person in the eye. Only then can you tell the nature of the connection between the mouth and the mind, so to speak.

Not only did I like this young man, but at times I was a bit confused. He was so like his father that once or twice I half thought it was to his father I was talking. But that wasn't the only confusion. Feelings were stirring in me. Feelings that were fifty years old and should have been dead long since. It was strange, but it was as if the forty years with Paddy had never happened. I nearly had to pinch my arm to remind myself that I was sixty-nine, and not nineteen. I was being disloyal to Paddy. But, Lord save us, I was enjoying myself as I hadn't enjoyed myself in years.

Back in the lorry I settled down as if I had spent my life riding up and down the country in one of them. The sun was setting and the blue sky was promising a sharp frost. I found myself looking forward to the carol singing at Midnight Mass, and the children's excitement.

'We must get yourself and Dad together before you back down home,' my young friend said.

I'm sure my blood pressure soared just then, but I didn't care. After that my imagination went wild. What if the old attraction was still there? What would he look like? I felt I was still a handsome enough woman. I hadn't allowed myself to gain weight. But then, I hadn't brought good clothes with me, because of Maeve's pawing children. But maybe I could borrow something from Maeve. We were about the same size.

Before I knew it we were sailing up past Inchicore and Kilmainham. The view of the Royal Hospital was spectacular from the height I was at. Wouldn't that be a nice place for us to meet, I thought.

We were pulling in to Heuston with me feeling like a queen at the prow of a ship, just as Maeve and two of her children were getting out of the car at the other side of the road. The children spotted me climbing down from the cab, and were jumping with excitement and trying to focus their mother's attention on me.

Her face when she greeted me was a sight for sore eyes. 'Mammy, what in God's name were you doing in that thing?'

'It's none of your business at all, Maeve Moody,' I replied. The children were aghast.

Michael handed me a piece of paper and climbed back into the lorry before I had time to introduce him.

'I'll be in touch!' I shouted, as I stood and waved him off.

Maeve may have been hoping that none of her neighbours were around to witness this shame brought on her by her mother, but I was confidently looking forward to Christmas.

Burren memories

Bitter winds rip across Galway Bay.

A swell heaves and crashes its thunderous

power

On Black Head's stalwart bulk.

It stands heavy in half shadow,

Shouldered by rocks,

Whitened by sun,

Scored by torrents.

Ground down by ice.

A bullfinch perches near a berry,

Crimson for a moment against a white
boulder.
It flicks its tail, picks the fruit and flies
away.

A deserted house crumbles.
Fossils in lintels, smoke-stained hearth
Whisper of living in death's destruction.

A *cilin*, small and rounded,
On a sunlit hillside,
Spills secrets in the darkness of Limbo's
tale.

Goats prance.
Seagulls swoop.
Pine martens tumble behind a wall.

Corcomroe Abbey broods, still and grey.
Its Matins and Vespers buried now
In the deep vaults of history's chasm.
Its essence rings in time's memory

Of Burren lives

Lived

Butter

In another life
I made butter.
Thick yellow clods of it
Floated to the top of the milk.

And then the great lump
To be lifted
Kneaded,
Salted,
Tasted

In the basement dairy.

Leave no milk in it.

Squeeze it.

Wash it

'Till sweating beads of salty water

Glisten on its surface.

Shape it with wooden paddles

'Till ridges crisscross its fatty yellow.

The satisfying completion

Of nature sucked, slapped and shaped

For our delight

A wet world out there

A wet world out there.

Wind swipes gales

Through the grey morning.

New camellias, gowned in pink,

Wave their innocence

Against the tired winter's green.

Birds chirrup.

Three seagulls soar.

Crows in chaos swoop.

A pigeon flutters from bush to bush.

Uncertainty clouds a spring morning

As winter battles for supremacy.

Dogs curl in oblivion.

I relish the drama

Cherry blossoms

A death is happening now

Right outside my window.

Pink, demented snowflakes

Dance, frolic or rage

Against a wind

That rips the petals

From blossoms

That yesterday glowed

Under an April sun.

They drift now

Still lovely

Still pink

Awaiting death.

I close my eyes and pray for

Green shoots and

Rebirth

Do something !

AT FIRST the screams came in waves; now they were constant - an unbroken, shrill piercing of his head. He stuffed cotton wool in his ears. It worked, blotting out the sound.

Images replaced the awful noise - disturbing images. Images of a child naked in mud in the back garden; a woman naked at the bedroom window; a nine-year-old boy skulking, head bent on his way to school; men coming and going; older children coming and going.

There was no laughter in that house.

He took the cotton wool out. The screams had not stopped. They drilled and pierced the thin wall between their terraced houses. He moved to the kitchen, to slight relief.

The screams faded a little. Were they the screams of a hungry child? Milk might help. He drank a glass of milk. It eased the pain in his chest - the pain he got when he saw the boy who never smiled or the baby naked in the mud puddle.

'God give me a break!' he cried. He opened the back door. The screams grew louder. A head appeared at another neighbour's back door and vanished quickly. Heads were looking and listening. The screams lived in the top back bedroom. The window was open. The east wind blew its icy blades through the open casement. The child was cold.

The mother was not naked at the bedroom window. Her blond hair did not stream in countless silken threads over her delicate white shoulders. She was not inside the kitchen window with her cigarette dangling from her pursed lips. Maybe her rubber-soled boots were now padding their way up the front path.

He moved to the front of the house. Here the screams were faint - a normal child's crying; not the hungry, cold muddy shrieks from the back of the house. Not a sign of her.

He went inside. The radio would drown out the sounds. He switched it on. Music. Gay Byrne or Pat Kenny or Marian Finucane might help.

A child should laugh as well as cry. He was sure he had heard a psychologist say that on the Gay Byrne hour. Laughing is important. Crying is important - but not one without the other.

The woman neither laughed nor cried. He never heard her speak. But she smoked and stood naked at the back bedroom window. She leaned over once through the dark openness. Her breasts hung and shook. He opened his mouth and stared and imagined his head nestling in the soft, smooth warmth of their milkiness. But it was babies who did that. The music intruded. He switched the radio off.

The baby screamed and drilled its shrieks into the dry east wind. Where was the mother? Her soft milkiness was made for comfort - the baby's comfort.

'God, give me a break!' he choked. He moved to the front door. She would turn the corner at the bottom of the street, he hoped. The sun was low in the sky. He would see her legs through the thin gauzy fabric of her flowing skirt - legs that he knew ended in soft darkness below her belly.

He knew because he had seen it at the back bedroom window. She had shown it to him. She knew his sadness and had taken pity on him. She had turned her back and sat her creamy bottom on the window sill. He dreamt of her bottom nestling in the dark pit of his belly. The memory eased his pain.

At the front door the light streamed in and dazzled him. He walked down the path to the gate. Now he could hear no sound from the back bedroom. A car zoomed up the road and bumped heavily on the unexpected ramp. Neighbours had forced the council to put those ramps in. Children needed to play safely on the road. Parents needed to know that their children were safe from speeding strangers. Here, people cared about children.

He had never seen the boy play on the road.

A front door slammed shut. Footsteps fell on concrete. An unoiled hinge squeaked as the gate opened and shut.

He knew by the sound that it was three doors down. The woman there would be going to the shop for her milk and evening paper. She was old and stooped. She had grey curly hair and glasses - a bit like his mother before she died.

She had looked at the back bedroom window. 'Someone should do something about that woman', she said. 'That kind of thing should not happen in a Christian country.' She went on her way.

'Do something, do something, do something,' he repeated to himself as he turned and walked back to the front door. He saw the boy at the sitting room window. The boy looked at him. He had never before seen the boy's eyes. He had only ever seen him walk with his head down, close to the wall, sometimes hitting his body on it.

They were big eyes and they were looking directly at his. 'Do something,' they said. 'Do something.'

He stood paralysed looking into the eyes of the nine-year-old boy at the window. They were soft and pleading. The boy stood still looking through the glass at the man. The man stood still. Barriers lay between them. They were strangers; there was glass. Did the boy know his mother's soft milky breasts? Did he cushion himself on her dark warm lap?

A long and hard journey it was from the middle of his own path to the boy's front door. The boy opened the door and ruptured the womb of this man's isolation. Smells of filth and piss, baby's screams, a small boy's big pleading eyes.

'Where is your mother?'

The boy did not answer. He looked up at the man and handed him a note. It said, 'Gone to the pictures. Mind the baby.'

'Take me to the baby.'

Their footsteps on the bare boards of the stairs drowned the screams. The door of the back bedroom was locked. Smells of shit oozed through the cracks and holes in the door.

'Where's the key?'

The boy looked at him. His eyes were watery.

'Are you hungry? I can give you some milk.'

A shadow darkened the bright space of the open front door. It was the mother. Her legs outlined against the evening sun were fat and short, ending in flat, black laced up boots.

He descended the stairs and slowly saw her waist and chest and neck and head. Her pursed lips held a cigarette. Her skin sagged in loose pockets from her eyes and cheeks.

They looked at each other. She was passive and inscrutable; he was angry.

'Feed your children.'

She moved aside. He walked out the door. He turned before starting the journey back to his own front door. She too had turned to look at him.

'Feed your children,' he repeated more loudly than before. She shut the door and he returned home.

His chest hurt. He would drink milk.

Much later, in the silence of twilight, he went to the back of the house. The back bedroom window was shut. The curtains were drawn. There was no crying. He went back inside to watch the evening news.

Confusions

It was meant to be

A gallop away

From daily duties,

From impositions,

From a muddled pie

Of infinite confusions.

But seagulls screeched

Over muddied water.

A man called out my name

As ducks dived
Up-arsed in green muck.

A woman wore my earrings
In the ascenseur.
A camera breached security
And drew venom
That poisoned a good day.

Winds blew
Rains fell
A heron, elegant, furtive,
Stalked a fish.
Security stalked
Our walking dogs.

It was the early hours
Of a sunless, midsummer's day.
We packed our bags
And scurried back
To manageable confusions

Death of a shrew

It was just a little shrew

Sharp-nosed, plump

With four tiny legs

Rigid in *rigor mortis*

That stopped me dead

On a wet path.

Was it a well-fed cat

That teased and tipped

The shrew

Until in terror

It breathed

Its final breath

And

Like a whisper's
Last refrain
Fell dead
In the dark of night?

No mourning cries
No tinkling bells
No mumbled prayers
To mark its passage.
Just red rose petals
To cover it
Where I placed it
On brown wet clay
To rot in private.

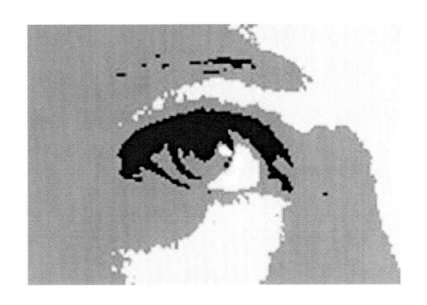

19 February, 2003

- the day Bush attacked Iraq

I see

A green lawn

Cut by a man

Against a bitter wind.

I see

A blackbird

Drag a worm,

Like elastic,
Out of black earth.

I see
Two dogs –
One black, one white.
In mock battle
They tussle.

A wintry spring in dull grey
Issues no invitations
To buds or daffodils.
Yet they come – uninvited,
Welcome to a year
That plods its newness
Across a frozen Europe
To Iraq.

Will they do it?
They won't dare.
Yes, they will.
Give them time.

Grief on grief beckons.

Sadness multiplies.

They stomp their boots

On squealing mice.

'We know best,' they say.

This mouse loves her dogs

And birds

And new green lawn.

She can do no more

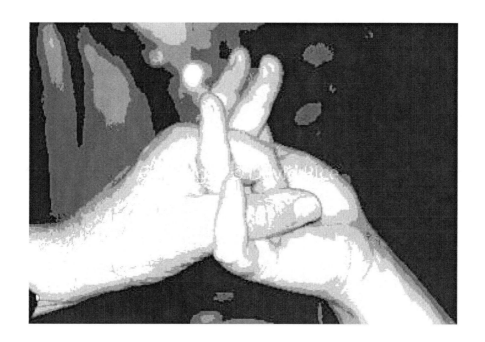

Hero

LITTLE John Ryan was beside himself with excitement. His tiny chest could hardly contain the pounding of his heart; his throat tightened every time he thought of his big brother, Tom. For Tom was his hero - 10 years older than he, a big strong man and now the hero of the entire countryside along with their friend, Paddy Sullivan.

Earlier that day word had come through on O'Beirne's phone that the pair had won the All-Ireland handball match in Roscrea. And now his brother was on his way home, to be greeted by the clapping and cheering crowds.

John had found himself a perch on the high wall across from the church. The street was at its widest here, and maybe the lorry carrying the heroes would stop there for a bit. Then he would get a good look at his brother, and maybe Tom would look at him and smile, and the whole world would know that this was his brother bringing glory to the parish.

Pigger Neilson would surely be impressed and stop calling him 'Flat Foot Freak'. After all, no Neilson had ever brought glory to Ballivore. And, to judge by his mother's 'huh' every time he mentioned Pigger's prowess at pitch-and-toss, maybe there were worse things than flat feet.

From his vantage point John was sure he would catch the first glimpse of the approaching lorry. It would come over the hill about a half mile out the road, and, if he was lucky, he'd be the first to see it and scream, 'They're coming!'

It was a magnificent evening. The sun was setting in a pool of pink light behind the hills across the lake. The day had been warm for early October, and now there was a hint of crisp cool autumn evening replacing late summer warmth. Would they ever come?

John couldn't make out why his father and mother wouldn't come to the village. The milking was over and the calves fed, and there was no reason at all why they couldn't come and enjoy themselves. But then they never did frequent the village except for the shopping, and selling the eggs at Brown's shop.

Far be it from him to fathom the depths of grown-up thinking. He was here himself, anyway, and never had his life seemed so blessed and happy. He'd walk tall for ages after this.

A familiar whistle at the other side of the street caught his attention. There was Pigger with his father, and brother, Sean. As usual Mr Neilson was drunk. How Pigger put up with the embarrassment of that spitting, foul-mouthed father, weekend after weekend, was beyond John's understanding. To be honest, John was more than a little afraid of Mr Neilson, and tried to avoid him when he was drunk. Even when sober, the man was silently hostile.

The distraction of Pigger's whistle had been enough to make him lose concentration, and just then Billy O'Rourke shouted, 'Here they are.'

Sure enough there was the red Commer, with headlights blazing and horn blaring, flying down the hill at great speed past the trees glowing in their pre-winter reds and yellows.

Even though John was raging that he hadn't been the first to spot the lorry, he quickly recovered from his disappointment and started screaming like the rest. This was heaven! For a second he thought he might make a complete eejit out of himself and burst out crying. But no, things were happening too fast. The lorry was in the village now, and there, standing proudly behind the cab, waving, laughing and shouting, were Tom and Paddy.

John's eyes were for Tom only, and what a joy it was to look at him. Not tall but handsome, dark and strongly built. He was wearing a white shirt and grey trousers - his Sunday best, and never did an older brother look so smashing.

Sure enough the lorry stopped at the church gates. Tom was waving and turning in all directions to acknowledge the crowds.

Then he saw John. He didn't just wave and call to him. He beckoned Oweny Ryan on the ground to do something. Before he knew it, John was lifted bodily off the wall and planted feet first over the wooden parapet of the rear of the lorry, straight into the arms of Tom.

Soon he was high over the crowd, with Tom's head in his hands and his legs dangling over his shoulders. He could see everything! What a crowd there was out there cheering for Tom.

This would put Pigger in his place. His older brother never achieved anything except maybe a black eye in a drunken brawl.

Deirdre Mallon was sitting on the wall at the corner of Delaney's bar. Her blond hair glowed in the last rays of the setting sun. She was a lovely sight - immaculate in her crisp flowery dress, brown legs dangling over the grey concrete. Usually when John saw her she was chatting in some group, always the centre of attention and never aware of his existence. It was different now. She had to see him on this lofty perch where, for once, his flat feet did not seem like duck's paddles anchoring his small frame to the ground. He was dizzy with excitement.

There was a brief lull in the shouting and cheering - the kind of pause you often get in conversations when someone says, 'Hush, an angel passing!' Then the lull was shattered by the raucous guffawing of some idiot near the lorry. Soon John realised that Pigger's father had his cap off and was waving it in the air shouting,

'And where's your fucking Blueshirt father tonight, Tom Ryan?'

The shouting seemed to grow louder and louder. All John could hear over and over again was, 'Fucking Blueshirts, fucking Blueshirts.'

John felt Tom's body freeze beneath him. It seemed to harden like iron, and then he found himself roughly thrust to the floor and Tom was leaping over the side of the lorry into the crowd.

It may only have taken seconds but it seemed that for hours Tom vanished into a mass of bodies with violently flaying arms and legs. The Gardai were quickly on the scene. One of them grabbed Tom by the back of the neck and frog marched him through the crowd down the street to the barracks.

Pigger's father was lying on the ground. He could have been dead. There was blood around his mouth and his face was horribly white with a kind of yellow glow around his eyes and nose. John felt fear and cold grip his whole being. It was getting darker by the minute and he was glad. He could scarcely believe that the cheering, happy crowd had so suddenly changed to a menacing, rumbling mob, from which he could catch comments like, 'You can't beat breeding', and 'Like father, like son.'

Tom was in disgrace. Any feelings of goodwill from the crowd were now directed towards Mr Neilson who was still stretched out on the ground. He was, however, beginning to show signs of life again.

John climbed down off the lorry and as quietly as possible slipped between the village houses and the crowd until he reached the gate that would give him a shortcut across the fields to the road up home.

He didn't feel safe until the last sounds of the village faded behind him and he was alone in the dark chill of this strange October evening. He was longing to be at home by the fire now. His father and mother would be settling down after the supper; he to smoke his pipe and just sit quietly, she to read a newspaper or a book.

Much as John wanted to be at home, he stopped, as he always did, at the gate of Reilly's field. From here he could see right back over the village, with its street lights now shining. The outline of the dark hills was etched against the remaining light in the western sky.

It was peaceful here but there was a new feeling lurking in his belly. Out of the confusing mass of thoughts and emotions battling within him was the clear awareness that maybe Mam and Dad were wise to stay at home and avoid the village. Their family was a little different from others. He couldn't think why, and didn't get much time to dwell on it because he could hear a car coming. It quickly shot past him but he had time to see that it was the local Garda car taking Tom home in disgrace.

He ran as fast as he could and reached his own front door almost as soon as Tom. His mother called from the fire, 'Hello, Love. You did well today.'

'Yes, Mam,' said Tom. ' But I'm tired. We'll talk about it tomorrow.'

With that, Tom climbed the stairs to bed leaving the kitchen quiet with the fire glowing and the kettle boiling. John sat beside his mother. The warmth of her body and the comfort of the kitchen gradually worked their magic, and the strange ache in his belly subsided.

An ordinary morning

(for Victor)

In a cool breeze

Branches bend,

Leaves flutter,

Cattle tails swat flies,

Swallows fly low.

An engine thrums a hollow sound.

I look and see and hear

But not as I did yesterday.

A cruel stroke,

A blinding stroke

On an ordinary morning in July

Has clipped life's wings

And splintered his before

Forever after

April 9, 2009

(for Johnny)

Grief groans in hollow emptiness

It wrenches memories

Of a baby's woolly wrapping,

Of childish tumbles in fields of hay,

Of a million silly things

That dream you back

From death's devouring power

On an innocent spring morning

That forever makes April

Home to your birth and death.

Archway

Oblivious to roaring trucks
Or the traffic's thrumming beat
He stands agape,
    at the edge of the road
Thin limbed,
    sledge hammer poised,
Intent on his task.
It was just an archway –

last vestige
   of an old gateway
Just a relic
   of ancient history

With all the strength of his puny might
He draws a blow.
Metal bounces on stone.
He jumps back.
The archway blows
A puff of dust,
But stands unmoved,
Splendid, beautiful,
Uselessly defiant
Against the anger
Of the ganger's timekeeping.

We all zip by
Cars, buses, trucks
Unaware or aware
Of time's echo
In a fleeting moment

Auntie Joan's first anniversary

A ghostly shroud

In voile

Covers the hills.

Houses loom,

Shadowy white,

Through the cold air.

A yellow digger,

In a field,

Paralysed

In dampness,

Bows,

Arm bent

At two elbows.

Raindrops shimmer

On a drooping branch.

A robin flicks his tail

In defiance

Against the stillness

Of this bitter morning.

Your voice echoes back to me

From a telephone conversation,

Life is precious,

Life is precious.

A worm rises to earth's surface.

A yellow blackbird beak

Grabs its opportunity

On the morning

Of the first anniversary

Of your sudden Death

Periwinkles in Lahinch

I swear I could smell the sea
As soon as we rounded the bend
At Ennistymon.

Seaweed and shells on roundy rocks
And yellow sand –
I would build castles in Lahinch
With my new, shiny bucket and spade.

A pipe band played music.

Men all dressed in skirts

Blew airs from Scotland

And tunes from Ireland

Through the screechy excitement of salt

wind

And chasing children

And ice-cream cones and candyfloss

And sticky pink peppermint rock.

After lunch my mother slept.

She gave me a tanner for periwinkles.

The woman rooted fistfuls

Of salty sea snails

Out of a rusty bucket

And filled a cone made of newspaper.

Time and patience,

A straight pin and the knack

Brought a long juicy, fleshy morsel

To delight the taste buds of a true

connoisseur.

I kept a few for my mother.

But she didn't wake up on time.

I ate them too.

And then there were rashers for supper.

The wild, sunny, gasping joy of it all

And the freezing sea.

But the periwinkles

Were from heaven

Armoured car

A grey armoured car
blocks the road.
Bulky, impenetrable,
Studded sheets of steel
encase its occupants
in safe seclusion
or isolation.

A missile strikes.
Armour shatters to brittle fragments

And thereby calls aloud

To ears that hear:

Safety is the illusion

That belies

The chains

The walls

The precepts

That bind, protect or halt

The free flight of

Love's infinity

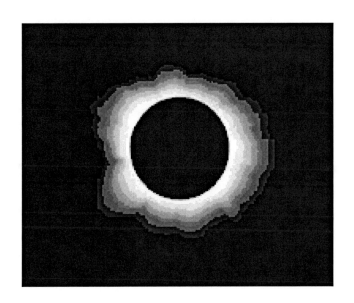

Eclipse

9 January 2011

Just for a while

The moon

Bit a bite of sun.

The world gazed

And wondered.

We wondered

At the darkness.

We wondered

At the precisions

And configurations

Of the universe's

Timings and tunings.

We looked and wondered

Long into the morning.

Sometimes I wonder

And gaze

At a world

Grief bitten and dark.

Not yet restored to living light.

Yet knowing time's

Attunement

To restoration

Shadow of a crow

I MET you once. You were fifty-nine then and you were dying. My mother asked me to visit you in the Mater Hospital. You sat up in your bed and greeted me, the daughter of your old friend. Your eyes sparkled. Mascara and eye-shadow heightened their vivid blue, and I was in no doubt about your pleasure in seeing me.

I had grown up knowing your name and imagining who you were and why they always called you 'poor Kitty'. Your sisters never referred to you. There were secrets surrounding you.

You lived in Dublin. My mother slipped off on the train sometimes to visit you. She'd come back with presents for all of us and I'd hear her tell my father that Kitty was in good form. They'd chat about your job in the laundry, and how you had made your life there and how one particular nun had been good to you and you were happy now.

I was too young then to bother much about you or why you were in Dublin and never came home, or why your sisters didn't seem to know you existed, or why I was warned never to mention your name outside of our family.

I remember once my mother telling my father that you and she had gone to the Gresham Hotel for tea. You stopped at the doorway and she said, 'I can't go in there, Mary. That's not for me.'

My mother rounded on you and said, 'Isn't our money as good as the bishop's?'

Later that night my mother said to my father, 'I wouldn't mind only she was better dressed and more beautiful than many of the bun-guzzling brigade already in the lobby.'

You went in and enjoyed your tea and I often wondered was that a turning point in your life. I hope it was.

That day in the hospital you asked me a strange question. You said, 'Did a flock of crows ever pass over you on a sunny day and drop their shadows down on you?'

I said, I didn't think so.

Your eyes grew wide. Emotion welled up from the depths of your remembering. Was it grief or love or hurt? I don't know. But you looked through the thin skin of my inexperience and told my soul - I've known things you couldn't possibly know.

'It happened to me once when I was cycling to the bog in Annaholty,' you said. You turned you head away then. It was time to leave you.

I know now about the bog and what happened to you there.

It was in June, wasn't it - a perfect day for turf cutting? You loved the bog. You loved the bicycle ride there with the sun shining, the yellow furze glowing in the hedges and the rhododendron flashing purple on the black peat. The ground was still wet enough to ease the probings of the slane. But it would be heavy for lifting.

Footing was your job. You were strong and willing in your flowery dress and big flat shoes. Your brown, permed hair clung stiff and tight to a head that seemed too small for your tall body. I've seen photographs of you from that time.

The boys were already there as you cycled down the narrow bog lane. You saw their bicycles thrown against the bushes. Did you wonder if Peter Touhy had arrived? You knew he was home on holidays from university. Did you know his bicycle so well that your heart skipped a beat at the sight of it lying there?

He was handsome. His father was rich. He was the heart's desire of all the girls in the parish and you had reason to believe that he fancied *you*. The Touhy family turf bank was beside yours. Hogan's was a little further away but near enough for lunch-time picnics together.

Paddy Hogan shouted when he saw you, 'Peter, Peggy's here.' Someone whistled. You were embarrassed.

Your father looked up from his cutting and glared through you. You ran to where he had already started tossing up the black bricks of winter fuel. Last week's sods were dry enough for footing, and you grabbed the wheelbarrow. Your hands, like your feet were big and strong. They worked at their lifting and building of heaps of turf 'til your nails were black and your veins ran purple through your yellow-stained skin.

Your father was a hard man. He worked you like a donkey lest you get ideas above your station.

Your brothers didn't come to the bog that day. They were at a fair in Nenagh. Your father would leave early to collect money from them at the Yellow Bridge pub.

They would come home late, drunk, hungry, abusive and possibly violent. You and your mother would have to prepare mountains of food to quell their appetites. But now was not the time to be thinking about that.

The sun was shining. Peter was only yards away and the Hogans were there. There would be fun before the day was over.

Stooping to pick up the sods was back-breaking work. Your father had little sympathy. He eyed you often during the morning – more than usual you thought. What's on his mind, you asked yourself. My mother told me of your sadness at never having had a conversation with him during his entire life.

In turn you eyed him as you rose to drop the sods in the wheelbarrow. Like you, he was tall and thin. His old grey suit hung on him like rags on a scarecrow. An ancient black trilby sat jammed down on his head, defying any wind to shift it.

Did you think of the crow shadows when you looked at him? Did you wonder were they a bad omen? My mother told me you were superstitious about crows. Did your father's shadow stretch long and thin towards you across the turf and dried heather?

You worked in silence until lunch break. You didn't mind the work or the silence. You could look forward to the picnic lunch.

The water in the small stream on the other side of the lane was clear and cool. You dipped your feet. Its freshness eased your aching muscles. You cleaned your hands. You sat and felt the heat of the sun on your back.

A black thread stuck to your foot. You knew what it was. But you had never before seen them here. There were plenty of them in the Mill River at home. You called them eels but they were blood-suckers and stuck fast to the skin of any foot that came their way. You pulled it out and thought no more of it.

You were hungry. You took the lunch box from the basket on your bicycle and headed towards the usual picnic spot with the Hogans and Peter. Your father growled, 'leave it there', indicating a place on your own bank.

They had already gathered. The fun had started. But you knew better than to defy your father. What was he up to? What did the others think? Paddy Hogan called out something but didn't finish it. They all went silent.

You settled your own picnic on the driest patch you could find. You sat and wondered and felt the heaviness of grief for a day gone sour in the shadow of your father's power. You ate your bread. It turned to dry lumps of dough in your mouth. You drank great gulps of cold tea to ease their passage to your stomach. Your father took his food and turned his back on you. He would not sit. His tall figure stood outlined against the sunlight, and you were glad you didn't see his face.

Did you hate him then, Peggy? Or did you hope for a miracle that would make him say, 'I'm sorry, love, go on over to them and enjoy yourself.' He threw the crusts of bread out beyond the bog-hole and into the dried heather scrub. Crows swooped from nowhere and fought for the free pickings in the dead wood.

In no time at all you were both back at work. He dug with the energy of madness at the black peat and threw up mounds of slippery sods that would be dry for next week's footing.

Peter and the Hogans returned to work quickly too. Your father's black mood had clearly stretched to descend on them. Soon everyone was back to the rhythmic bending, lifting, wheeling and digging of that afternoon in the bog.

Suddenly your father jumped up over the bank he was working on. His face had energy in it and it was focused on you.

'I'm goin' to the Yalla Bridge. Finish your work here and stay away from them,' he said pointing, at the Hogans.

You would do as you were told. You stood and watched your father stride towards the bicycles. He found his, and, like a man with serious purpose, mounted it and rode at speed up the bog lane.

You knew what that meant. He had money and alcohol on his mind and it would be a hard night for you and your mother.

You turned and saw that the Hogans and Peter had watched every move. You went back to work wondering why your father had said, 'Stay away from them.'

The heat was getting to you as you wheeled one of the last barrowfuls of sods. You would soon be finished. You would go to the stream again for the comfort of its cool water. The blood-suckers didn't matter. You knew how to deal with them. You stacked the sods and turned the barrow for the last load. The two Hogans were coming in your direction.

We're off for a smoke,' Paddy said. 'Go on over to Peter. He wants you.'

You looked towards Peter and saw him behind one of the taller furze bushes. He beckoned you towards him. You heard your father's warning, stay away from them. But why would you need to stay away from Peter? You loved him and you thought he liked you. Joy rose in you and you dropped the handles of the barrow. You wiped your hands on your skirt and walked towards him.

You looked back to check that your father had gone. The Hogans were walking on the lane but there was no sign of your father.

Peter seemed impatient. His face was red and had a strange look on it. 'Come on, Peggy,' he said.

'What do you want me for?' you asked.

'Come and sit beside me for a while.'

'There's nowhere to sit.'

Something was wrong. You were wary. You should run away. Peter was strange, not himself. You sensed danger but he grabbed your hand and said, 'Lie down'. He pushed you and you fell on the dried out heather and furze. You screamed from the pain of the furze spikes stabbing your back.

He was breathing heavily, eyes glazed, looking at you, but not looking at you. His teeth bit at your lips and tongue as he forced his mouth over yours. He groped at your breasts with rough, dirty hands. How would you explain your dirty, torn dress to your mother? He pulled at your knickers and held you down with one hand on your breastbone. He fumbled with the buttons of his trousers. You had no breath to scream. Your back burned with the pain but that was nothing to the pain between your legs as he drove a hot rod into your belly.

Peter, you're hurting me,' you managed to say through your shock and terror.

'You shut up about this,' he replied. 'I'll kill you if you ever mention my name.'

It was over and he was gone.

My mother cleaned you up that evening. You told her the story and bound her to secrecy. She honoured that secrecy until you were dead and buried. It was only then that she told me about your day on Annaholty bog and of the baby born in that home in Dublin. It was adopted in America and you were sentenced to life imprisonment in *THE MAGDALEN LAUNDRY*.

God rest you, Peggy, and all the women whose love and innocence condemned them to the cruelties of the virtuous.

That hour of night

It is that hour of night
When nothing happens.
Life lies still,
Aware, fearful,
Hungry for action
For solutions
For resolutions.
Phones don't ring.
Lights are quenched.

Night bathes in the quiet flow

Of seconds filling minutes,

Of anxious deliberations

And suppositions

Or propositions.

Life ebbs or flows

Or, like the river

Roars in endless whirling pools

Of all-consuming

Black turbulence

To mighty endings

And new beginnings

An acorn

My friend planted an acorn
  Right way up
 In a pot of rich compost
From a midland bog.
She carefully bedded it,
  Firmed it down,
Watered it and placed the pot
On the sunny side of the garden.
In Spring a green shoot
  Poked its nose

Through the soft, black surface
Of the precious pot.
We looked, admired and gently touched
  The delicacy of its new green life.

It grew small thin arms
  With leaves greenly testing,
Playing in a sunny breeze.

She nourished, watered
  And tended its youth
Until stronger arms
Waved confident twigs
Against wet west winds.

But the wind being wet
  Cold and stormy
Blew spores of illness
  Death and destruction
Into the deepest folds of
Green new shoots.

What had we left undone

That undid the acorn's

Power to survive

And become a majestic oak?

An ordinary day

It was an ordinary day
For walking the hills
Through the swish and wave
Of pine and larch
In the deep, dull tune
Of a creaking forest.

Head bent, intent,
I trod on shimmering mica
In the glinting granite
Of the Dublin hills.

Then

He was there,

All angle-antlered

Right before me

In a sunny place.

Stunned to awe,

Or was it fear?

We stared.

I blinked.

He was gone

To the dark confusion

Of tangled trees.

While I, in light,

Marched on

Through the forest's freeway

Into a new

Extraordinary day

St Martin and the geese

DID you know that St Martin of Tours was the patron saint of Geese? Why should geese need a patron saint, I hear you ask. The answer I believe lies not so much in any need the geese might have had but rather their role in an important event in the life of this venerable saint

I was reminded of this recently when I read a book by Mr Kevin Griffin of Ballina, Killaloe. The book relates to a section of the parish of Ballina called Boher. But it was the references to Curraghmore, a townland of Boher, that caught my attention. This is the area that so many of my ancestors came from.

My grandmother, Johanna McGrath, was born there in the year 1885. She lived in the ancestral home there until her marriage to John Quigley of Grange, Ballina, in 1916. A distance of only four miles separates the two townlands but in those years such a distance meant the separation of two quite different cultures.

My grandmother was a woman of strong will and, instead of studying and following the traditions of her new area, she brought some of the ancient practices of her native end of the parish with her.

I was probably about four years of age when I witnessed her performance of one of these rituals. My memory may be a bit sketchy but I clearly recall her bending at the front door of her farmhouse. She held a full sized goose under her arm and cut its neck with what I presume was a very sharp knife. She then poured the blood against the jamb of the door.

I remember being amazed at what I saw. I presume I asked several questions. But apart from the ritual itself, I can remember nothing other than her explaining it was something she had to do on St Martin's Eve.

Today's sensibilities would feel repulsed and indignant at such butchery being enacted before a small child. I hasten to add that I was not traumatised by the event. The slaughtering of animals *in situ* was a necessity in those days and I am sure my attention was instantly absorbed by other diversions.

Years later I became acquainted with a book called *The Lives of the Saints*. In it I found a chapter on the life of St Martin of Tours and there was the connection between Martin and the geese.

Martin was the son of a Roman military officer in the 4th century. He converted to Christianity in his teens and became an ardent believer. His reputation for holiness spread throughout France where he worked in a Roman garrison.

Such was his zeal that when the bishop of Tours died in 371, Martin was chosen to replace him. But this was not what the devout Martin wanted. He preferred the simple life of a hermit in the monastery he had founded near Tours. Legend has it that he hid in a barn to escape his zealous supporters. But a gaggle of squawking geese near there gave the game away on him. He was discovered and whisked off to the city where he was consecrated bishop on July 4th, 372.

Now, imagine the distance in miles between Curraghmore and Tours. Imagine also the distance in time: 1600 years! And yet, there was my grandmother in 1947 taking revenge on a poor goose for its ancestral betrayal of Martin of Tours.

It is interesting to speculate and wonder how this story – probably apocryphal anyway – came to be commemorated with such devotion by a people so far removed in time and space from its origins. Perhaps an Irish priest, educated in France in unhappy times, told the story to his captive audience of parishioners around the feast of St Martin – thereby giving everyone a good excuse for the first roast-goose dinner of the winter season. Who knows?

Martin, no doubt, in the true spirit of Christianity, forgave the geese, and in so doing merited the grand honour of becoming their patron saint.

To death's beginning

A new moon shimmers in a black sky.

A new rose buds on an old stalk.

The root that birthed a thousand blooms

Defies the gnarled death of winter's depths

To loosen the juicy freshness

In a bud so small

Its blood red petals hesitate

To grasp the warmth of spring's new sun

And join the riotous living

Of summer's symphony to life.

Cycles in circles wind us

And bind us to living

Springing us forever

From joyous birthing

To death's beginning

Freedom

Freedom speaks volumes

From the safe seclusion

Of a prison cell.

Let me in, one speaks

Let me out, another shrieks.

No meeting of minds

Can break the walls of cells

So thick and prejudiced

That not even the light of day

Or intuition

Or moral fibre

Or reason

Can sprinkle the dew

To loosen the spores

Of deathly, arid grit.

Granite stones

Worn vestiges of an ancient life

In the molten rumblings and explosions of

Earth's inner vibrancy.

Granite stones

Now rounded by weather,

Rusted by rain,

Yellowed by lichen,

Strewn amongst briars,

Heaped into walls

To house cattle, sheep or people.

It all adds up

To a green peace

In Connemara

Love

Love is not reasonable.

It is the madness

That breaks the boundaries

Of my lazy, couldn't-care-less

Humdrum ordinariness.

It takes me through the morning's

Chores of feed-the-dogs

Feed-the-birds

Water-the-plants.

Love is the summer sun's magic

That draws and licks the green earth's
juice
To make a poppy or the oak.
It is the hope that breaks the mould of
Could-not, would-not, should-not
Chains of despair.

Love is the yellow primrose
It is the red poppy
It is the blue sky
It is the green pea
It is the light that shines
Through the bleakest night
Before the dawn of hope

Pain

Pain grips

Clamping its jaws

Irrationally,

Nationally,

Internationally.

A viper head

Snaps its opportunities.

In confusion

Venom oozes,

paralyses.

A man beheaded
A child neglected
A woman agonised
A family fragmented
In disillusionment.

Rippling circles
Engulf them.
Drowning, they gasp
For time to understand,
For love to heal the pain,
For peace to settle storms.

A dog shakes its black wet coat.
I contemplate –
The deep blueness

A stick to steer with

We broke the teacher's stick
She and I.
No, *I* stole it
I broke it
And threw it over a garden wall.
The teacher interrogated her pupils.
Wide-eyed they looked.
I blushed.
She looked at me.
I looked at her.

We kept our counsel.
The storm passed.

I still break sticks –
Sticks that have beaten me,
Shamed me,
Driven me to guilt-racked wakeful nights.
Sticks that demanded blind obedience to
'We know what's good for you'.

Sticks of duty
To unnecessary duties bound.
Sticks of loyalty
To misplaced honour driven.

But now I seek another stick –
An oar,
A rudder
That I alone will steer
With a pure, cold wind
At my back.
And God-knows-what before me

The half-acre

THE thud of each shovelful of clay on your coffin exploded a hollow grief in me. That sound, more than any thinking or talking, placed you out of my reach forever.

I watched them cover the brass plate with dirt. Was that all that would remain of you in a hundred years, in a thousand years? A name,

Mary Ellen Coughlan, died August 6th, 1975, aged 75.

I had known you for many of those years. You were my godmother, my friend, and my life's blessing. Would anyone looking at your gravestone in a hundred years feel your fears, know your loves, or care about your hates?

I care. I will look your fears in the face. I want to live your loves and hates, and bury them in Inchabawn, where the great passions of your small life buried you in an isolation as tight as the tiny space that is your home forever now.

I will etch them on the being of that place. The wind will know your name, and rush it through the trees in nights of raging storms. The sun will bake your furies on the scent of heather and furze and dried-out peat. The passer-by will feel your fear in the flowing mists; hear your screams in the raven's croak; smell your witch's brew in black wet peat.

Were you a witch, Mary Ellen? They said you were. But they'd say anything. Even as a little girl, long before I was heard of, you knew the wild strawberries, wild peas, sorrel, and clover that grew on the stone walls, and in the fields.

Years later you taught me how to see them. You taught me how to feel your excitement at the first glimpse of a snowdrop. 'Look at the white of it,' you'd say, holding one up for me to see. 'Pure as God's grace in a budding year. Pure as a bride on her wedding day.'

'Look at the strawberry – the sun turns it red like your skin.'

I'd roll around laughing, and ask you would I get redder if I ate the strawberries. We feasted on them at every stone wall, from Inchabawn to Drumbwee.

'That's a fairy tree,' you'd say, when we looked through the pink blossoms of a hawthorn at the blue sky.

I searched for fairies there. 'They'd be dancing reels and jigs there on a Winter's night,' you told me.

A bad witch would not have taught me these things. Were you a good witch, Mary Ellen?

What is a good witch? Not the kind that mixes squashed beetle in her father's stew. You told me you did that.

You had good reason. Your father had seen death in the birth of his daughter. Death of his name. His beloved land would wither and die in the hands of a neighbour's son. A daughter did not count.

Your mother prayed for the birth of a boy. He came six years too late to ease the pain between you and your father.

'Mikey was a good little boy,' you told me.

'Stop fillin' that child's head with rubbish,' your father told you, when Mikey searched for fairies under the hawthorn bush.

Mikey learned the plough, the harrow, the scythe and knew a good cow from a bad cow.

'Mary Ellen is a bad cow,' you heard him tell a man on his confirmation day. You were seventeen then and well-schooled in the business of rearing pigs, chickens and making butter.

'Why did Mikey call me a bad cow?' you asked your mother.

'Don't mind him,' she answered. 'The half-acre field will be yours someday. My father gave it to me and I'm giving it to you.'

'I'd like a nice dress, Mama,' you said. 'Maybe I could go to the dance in Kelly's barn.'

Your mother looked at you pityingly, and said, 'Dances aren't everything, Mary Ellen.'

But the dress was made; the night came and you cycled to Kelly's barn. You stood near some girls you knew. They giggled and tittered. You sat and looked. Boys looked you over and you looked away. A pain entered your soul then. You howled that pain to the trees and stones as you cycled home.

'But I'll have the half acre field,' you told yourself and you felt a little better.

'Did you have a good time?' your mother asked from her soft feather bed.

'A lovely time,' you lied. And the world of dances and dancing died in you that night.

Mikey loved the dances. For a while you were 'Mikey Coughlan's sister,' and the girls talked to you on the village street. They'd ask, 'How is Mikey?' They'd gather round and tell you, 'He's a grand brother to have. Did he get a new suit lately? He looked smashing on Sunday night.'

The girls eyed you and you looked grim faced. You knew what they were thinking – how did he manage to get a sister like that?

When you got home you looked at Mikey with furrowed brow and the flared nostrils that you often had when you spoke of him. You hated him.

And you hated him on the night of your father's funeral, when he strutted and held himself tall and drank stout with the men. His was the strut of a king who speaks, 'I've come into my power now, and woe betide anyone who thwarts me.'

Your mother whimpered, 'I want Mary Ellen to have the half-acre field.'

But you saw the half acre with its little barn vanish from your grasp. A rage grew in you – a rage that bound you to that place like roaring gargoyles on church gables.

You worked a slave's day, year in, year out, on the side of that mountain. You bent to the rhythm of bluebell springs, rose-scented summers, yellow autumns and grey cold winters.

The night your mother died you said to Mikey, 'The half acre field is mine, Mama gave it to me.'

'It wasn't hers to give,' he answered. He knew the law just as you did. Women didn't exist in those hallowed halls of male importance and possession.

But you had other powers. Your time would come.

You loved the well in the callow field. Bottomless, you told me, and I believed you. You threw stones in there and I watched them vanish in the mud. 'They'll come out down in Australia,' you told me, and I believed you. I saw Australia and our stones falling from the sky. Some little girl there would pick them up and throw them into her well. Maybe they'd come back to Inchabawn before the next new moon.

'Make a wish,' you'd say. 'When a stone comes back you'll get your wish.'

I wished for everything under the sun – a puppy dog, a nice new dress, a baby sister. There was no end to my wishing.

What did you wish for ,Mary Ellen? You never told me. But you prayed at that well. You looked at your image mirrored in the water, and I knew that image would travel to Australia to find your longings and bring them back.

On your burial day you lay cold in your coffin, wrapped in frilly white silk. I thought of snowdrops and cold wintery fields. I thought of Mikey and the night he came home and told you, I'm getting married soon. You'll have to get out of the house and fix yourself up in the barn.'

The rage of your pent up life asked sweetly, 'And who's the lucky girl?'

Mikey's face relaxed then, and he said, 'Maura Cummins - you know her – a good woman.'

'And will you help me in my move to the barn?' you asked meekly.

'Yea, it's warm out there. You'll be all right. I'll get a carpenter to do a few things.'

You put Mikey at his ease. There was no battle. You'd move out. Maura would move in, and take over your scrubbed kitchen table, your hearth and Mama's wedding dishes.

You'd be grand and happy in the barn you assured him. Wouldn't it be the same distance to the pig-sty and the hen-house, as from your mother's kitchen? No trouble at all.

Maura would need running water and electricity. She was used to them. Couldn't do without them. You watched plumbers and electricians transform the kitchen, and you marvelled at every new change.

You visited the well often then. 'I love the well water,' you said to Mikey when he reminded you that you had a tap in the kitchen now. 'Sure isn't it God's miracle itself, that well, seeping in abundance out of God's good earth?'

You prayed at the well. You prayed at the four corners of the half acre. You planted trees in each corner. You dropped stones in the well.

And you waited.

'Maura is coming to look at the place,' Mikey said one day. 'Will you make a sup a tay for her?'

'Oh, isn't that great. Of course I will,' you replied.

You washed the best china tea set. You boiled the freshest eggs. You cooked the leanest piece of bacon.

'A feast fit for a king,' Mikey said when he saw it.

The fire glowed in the hearth, the new electric kettle bubbled with water from the well in the callow field. Maura sniffed and smiled. It was to her liking. She wore a green costume that day and you said, 'Green becomes you, Maura.'

Green is God's colour, you often told me. 'God likes green,' you'd say.

Mikey was your friend then. In the barn he moved oat bins and pulpers and bags of barley. A nice big room was prepared for his sister. There were shelves and a dresser. The settle bed from the kitchen fitted nicely under the window. The old fireplace for boiling pigs' food would be your new hearth.

'Oh, it's lovely,' Mikey you said. You visited the well every day. You sipped its water, and spoke God's words: 'In the name of the Father, the Son, and the Holy Ghost.' You walked the half acre from corner to corner, and you prayed to your mother's spirit for protection.

Your foot stuck in the wet peat of the half acre one day. You felt it suck you down and you knew you'd be safe.

'Maura's gone to hospital,' Mikey said one Friday evening. 'She's been poorly for a while.'

A silence drifted into the house – the silence of Maura's dying; the silence of Mikey's sighing; the silence of your triumph in the deep still waters of the callow well.

Whispers echoed from one end of the parish to the other. The Cummins's never had TB. "Twas never in them. Why did Maura get it?'

'It's that witch!'

'She was never normal.'

'What does she do all day long?'

'That witch brought it on. Maura got sick after visiting that house.'

Mikey heard the whispers and began the long slow journey to his own death.

You heard the whispers too, but they didn't touch you. Your work shielded you from staring eyes and busy tongues. I became your only contact with the outside world. I brought you bluebells and roses and you seemed happy.

'It's yours now – half acre and all,' you said to me before you died.

I was grateful, and promised that your story would be told to my children and their children's children. I pray that yours and your mother's spirit will bless its new life in a neighbour's name, and that the callow well will honour your longings in other lives.

Zest

I pared a lemon

This morning,

Down to its soft

Rubbery flesh.

Flesh that bends

And bruises,

Dries up

And withers

In a day.

Without its zest

And cover-up

Death comes quickly.

Just sometimes

Just sometimes I feel the need

To have about me more than I could ever

use.

I feel the need to live a life

Of ease and peace amid the strife of living.

I feel the need to gad about

And shout to scorn our rules and

regulations.

I feel the need to love the song
To sing it long on freely soaring wings.

I feel the need to save the world
From tears and deeds of demons driven.

I feel the need to bury my head
To hide or run from slights imagined,
From gossip charged, from illness
weakened.

Mostly though
I bumble along

Outside my window

Finches, sparrows, robins

And wrens are there.

Pecking, flapping or hopping.

They scurry

In endless pursuit of food,

Of warmth,

In fun or in fear.

Cats are there

Skulking, crawling,

Fat-bellied bullies
In endless pursuit
Of inbred obsessions.

Dogs are there.
Wolves by any other name,
Barking, scratching,
Protesting.
In endless pursuit
Of packed excitement.

Rats, gnats or brats
Come or go.
They play out their dramas
In comic, tragic
Committed
Pursuit of living
Outside my window

Autumn morning

Red fuchsia sways and tumbles
In a cool gust from the Southwest.

An orange leaf floats and falls.
It joins the sticky mulch on a grey road.

A seagull rises from a green field
And vanishes in mists rolling from hills.

Vestiges of russet linger on branches
Soon to be sticks and skeletons in the
death of winter.

Finches descend on orange berries.
Their fierce competition belies abundance.

A car horn blasts impatience
At a lingering slowing of the daily tempo.

The river churns, whirls and drags its load.
In scorn it roars its wintering power.

A cormorant, black as night, stands aware,
alert,
Alone on a buoy in mid river.

Along the jetty, boats are resting,
Asleep in an autumn morning.

The world stretches its limbs.
It awaits the dead of winter

Going home

SISTER Mary Benedict thought a lot about going home these days. Ever since Mother General announced that the overseas sisters could make a trip to visit their relatives, she thought of little else.

She had written a letter to her sister, Polly, to tell her the good news. She was expecting a reply any day now. It wasn't that she had ever forgotten Ireland. Throughout her sixty odd years in Madras, the memory of the soft Irish mists and the rain on the wind which drenched herself and her sisters on the way home from school, had often eased the scorching heat and withering dryness of her Indian convent.

Even today as she sat in the shade of the hot cloister, she had but to close her eyes to see Slieve Donn, with its quilt of violet rain clouds. The westerly winds would sweep them down across Lough Derg, to release their burden over Kilmurragh.

When people commented on her wonderful skin, which still had the softness and bloom of her younger years, she believed it was the wet winds and rains of her dreams that worked a miracle in this alien land.

And then there was her family. Her sister Polly was the eldest. She had married late in life, and was now a childless widow living in Kilmurragh. Peg, as Sister Benedict was known at home, was still a little in awe of this sister of hers. Polly had been the decision maker of the family. Giver their parents' milder natures, she had assumed responsibility for family discipline at an early age.

Peg could still remember the night she went on her bicycle over the hill to a dance in Tonlough. She was having a great time when Poll arrived to take her home.

'You're too young for this,' Poll had said. 'Mama and Dada didn't know what they were letting you off to.'

Peg still smiled to herself at the memory of Poll's face when Peg dug her heels in and said she would't go home. Indeed, to spite Poll, she had stayed out two nights at her friend's house.

Polly had worked all her life behind the counter of Conlon's shop, a job Peg herself would have loved. But such jobs were scarce in those days.

Then, when Peg was about sixteen, in her last year at school, two nuns came to tell the pupils of her school about their work in India, and how they needed more girls to join them. Peg was fired with enthusiasm by their description of schools and orphanages, and said so to Poll when she got home from school.

That night from her bed in the loft, she listened to Poll talking to her parents in the kitchen:

'Wouldn't it be a marvellous thing for her to do?' Poll had whispered. 'She's no beauty, God knows. Wasn't it hard enough getting a job for Jude in Brown's? And there's still Bella to be settled.'

Peg heard her mother sighing, and her father said nothing at all. But Peg knew in that moment that her future was mapped out for her.

It was only a few months later that her father died. He keeled over suddenly in the haggard, while forking hay. They were all beside themselves with grief. But it didn't stop Poll from taking her aside in the graveyard and saying, 'Now you'll have to join the convent. It's what you told Dada you would do.'

Peg felt unable to argue with this, because she too believed it would have been wrong to shame the dead, especially poor Dada whom she loved dearly. And besides she did think she was called to this work in India. The nuns had described it so well.

But that was all a long time ago. Mama was dead now and so was Jude. Polly and Bella were living in adjoining houses in the village, and they had both been great letter writers over the years.

Today, as she often did, Peg closed her eyes and in an instant was back in Kilmurragh. She could still see every house and shop and pub there. Some of the houses near the school were big two-storey buildings with railings and lovely lawns.

Even Marmalade, the tom cat that always sat sleeping on Murphy's wall, still purred and dribbled for her as, in her memory, she stroked its soft ginger fur. She had always loved when his rear end popped up as her fingers moved to the end of his spine. Peg had adored Marmalade because she could never stroke the cats at home.

They were wild – kept as rat catchers. Mama and Dada did not hold with making pets of them.

After Poll and Bella had sold the farm they bought two small houses near the railway station. They had no front gardens, but their back gardens were huge and took a lot of minding, they told her. They now employed the Gunner Leary's son to do a day's work for them occasionally.

Why, Peg wondered, had they bought two small houses instead of one bigger one, where they could have been happy together?

Anyhow, it would be lovely to see Kilmurragh again, and smell the clean fresh air from Slieve Donn. And maybe paddle in the river, and talk to people the way Mama did, coming home from the village with her shopping bags. Maybe they would ask her about her life in India, and she would think of interesting things to tell them. Then, maybe it wouldn't all seem so bad.

It would be lovely to go back in the summer, to the smell of hay and earth upturned with the digging of new potatoes. The green fields would be alive with flowers. The corncrake would be croaking from the meadow. And to see that spring well with its funny little flies hopping on the water.

Poll and Jude used to say there was no bottom to that well, and Peg had always taken care to step on the driest stones, not the slippery wet ones. Why had we never taken a stick to it to test its depth, she wondered now. We were so innocent in those days. She chuckled to herself.

She was startled by the ringing of the bell for Vespers. Oh dear God, she thought, why did I get so carried away? She usually made it her business to set out for chapel before everyone else, because the arthritis held her up so badly. Now she would be late.

Painfully she struggled to her feet, and made her way up the cloister to the door nearest the chapel. Once inside there was a handrail running the length of the corridor, and so she managed to move a little more quickly. On passing the pigeon-holes where Reverend Mother left the sisters' letters, she automatically glanced over. There, to her surprise, for she was not expecting it for another while, was the corner of a blue envelope sticking out over the edge.

She stopped for a second to catch her breath. She felt a tightening in her throat and for a while her breathing was difficult. No, she wouldn't cross the corridor to get the letter. She would wait until after Vespers, when she would have time to open it and read it quietly and privately, in her own room.

She continued to shuffle her way to the chapel and up to her prie-dieu. Her heart was beating with excitement, and when she could concentrate on the psalms, she found that this evening one had a new and special meaning for her:

> In meadows of green grass he lets me lie.
> To the waters of repose he leads me.
> There he revives my soul.

Normally she waited to say the Rosary after Vespers, but not this evening. On her way out Sister Clare stopped her and asked if she was feeling all right. Having reassured her friend, she all but bolted from the chapel door to the pigeon-hole. She snatched the letter and made straight, and not too painfully, to her own room. In the lift she was tempted to open it, but decided not to. She would wait until she had turned the key on the inside of her own door.

Downstairs Sister Clare was worried. She had never known her friend to leave the chapel in such a hurry. Neither did she look too well – maybe just a bit pale or even excited. However, an hour later, when Sister Benedict hadn't appeared in the refectory for supper, she went up to her room to check on her.

The door was locked, but its little old-style shutter yielded to her touch. She was able to push it back and turn the key.

Sister Benedict sat bolt upright in her chair, except that her head was bowed. On her lap, between her fingers, was a letter on blue paper.

Sister Clare took the letter and read the first lines: 'Dear Peg, Isn't it late in the day they decided to let you home? Bella and I have discussed it, and we concluded that there would be no point in your coming now. Everything has changed...'

Sister Clare had also come from Ireland many years ago and her loyalty to all the Irish sisters in the community was total. She stood for many minutes looking affectionately at 'Benny', as she called her. It wasn't difficult to work out what had happened. With a resolution that was both characteristic and final, she crumpled the letter and shoved it deep into her petticoat pocket.

What was in that letter was Benny's business and nobody else's. She turned and quietly left the room, went downstairs to tell Reverend Mother that Sister Benedict had passed away.

Does it matter now?

Does it matter now

That your words stung then

Like hot yellow mustard

On a child's tongue?

Or that your laughter

Shamed a young brain

Like egg yoke splashed

On a new red door?

Years have drained your venom

To atoms in solution

Or dissolution,

Until it matters now

Hardly at all

At all.

About the author

CATHERINE THORNE is a native of Ballina in the County of Tipperary, across the Shannon from Killaloe. In another life she taught French, English and Geography. Her passions are gardening, reading, her doggies, and writing poetry and short stories. One of her stories, *Fresh Bread*, was shortlisted for the Hennessy Award. She is a member of the Killaloe Writers' Group. This is her first published volume.

Lightning Source UK Ltd.
Milton Keynes UK
UKOW03f1235290914

239365UK00002B/67/P